Jokes for the John

IT'S A GAS MAN!!! For the perennially pooped, we offer you hormones in print. Someone has pulled our chain again, so relax, loosen your tie and get ready to yowl around like a hopped-up Tomcat.

Here, for your idle reading enjoyment is a new volume of lusty, gusty, and busty humor, that's been responsible for more blushes than an open zipper at an old maid's picnic.

This is the book that put the smoke into the clubcars. This is the book that Lolita is afraid to bring home to father.
This is the book that everyone out of their skulls are consulting their psychiatrists about.

In short, JOKES FOR THE JOHN is a collection of mental cathartics which have been carefully edited and re-edited to bring you ribald humor that is based on that provocative subject—SEX, which herein is twitted lengthily and uproariously, purely for the sake of adult entertainment.

Admittedly, there are many four letter functional words in this tome, words such as "don't", "can't", "won't", "stop", etc., but truthfully, they only add zest to the merriment.

For the man who has 'everything', this is a marvelous going away present, and should certainly keep him going for weeks.

When not in use, hang by its golden chain next to the rolled sheet music in your W.C. Your friends will look at you with admiration and ask: "Are you a nut or sumpthin?"

"Does your girl smoke?"
"Not quite!"

"Who's not having a good time?"

The little boy and his grandpa, who was a bit deaf, were watching the laughing hyenas at the Zoo. The attendant was telling the eager listeners that the hyena ate forty-five pounds of meat a week. Grandpa leaned over to his grandson and asked him what had been said. The boy repeated the fellow's remarks in his granddaddy's ear.

"The laughing hyena," continued the attendant, "is unusual because after digesting all that food, he usually evacuates only once a month." Again the grandfather asked his grandson to repeat what had been said which the boy did.

The old man thought it over for a moment and then snorted, "If that damn thing eats forty-five pounds of meat a week and only has one bowel movement a month, what the hell is he laughing about?"

"She won't be down—I hid her falsies!"

At an isolated part of the beach at Cannes a beautiful, young French girl threw herself into the sea. A young man off at a distance witnessed it and dashed into the water to save her. Unfortunately, he was too late. He brought the semi-nude body ashore and left it on the sand while he went to report the drowning. When he returned, he was horrified to discover a man making love to the corpse.

"Monsieur!" he exclaimed, "that woman is dead!"

"Sacre bleu!" exclaimed the man, jumping up, "I thought she was an American."

"Look! A girl!"

THIS IS A CHAIN LETTER

Dear Friend:
   This chain was started in the hope of bringing happiness to all tired business men. Unlike most chains, it doesn't require money. Simply send a copy of this to five male friends, then bundle up your wife and send her to the fellow whose name heads the list. When your name reaches the top of the list, you will receive 15,186 women and some should be dandies. Have faith. Don't break the chain. One man broke it and got his wife back.

      Your friend,
      Homebreakers, Inc.
Start Here:

A gorgeous girl walked into the psychiatrist's office. She no sooner closed the door, when the doctor ripped off her clothes and attacked her. After fifteen minutes, he got up and said, "Well, that takes care of my problem. What's yours?"

The old man walked into the drug store and said, "I'd like to get some of that stuff they give the fellows in the Army to make them forget about girls." The druggist, upon hearing this, said, "What would an old man like you want with stuff like that?" The old gentleman replied, "I wanna' stuff it up my nose and clear those ideas out of my head."

"He's a slogan writer and he says he has something that will fit me to a T."

"—Marilyn Monroe? —Gina Lollabrigida?
—Sophia Loren?—"

It was at the office Christmas party.
As they lay on the office reception
couch in the darkened room, their
breath came hot and fast.
"Oh, Melvin, Melvin," she said passionately, "you've never made love
to me like this before. Is it because
of the holiday spirit?"
"No," he panted. "It's probably because I'm not Melvin!"

Woman to dentist: I don't know
what's worse, having a baby or getting a tooth pulled.
Dentist: Make up your mind, lady,
I've got to know which way to tilt
this chair.

"Well, I can't think of a better way to go!'

The young man was determined to win his girl that evening.

"I have loved you more than you will ever know," he said.

"So I was right," she exclaimed, slapping him across the face. "You **did** take advantage of me last Saturday night when I was drunk!"

I'm looking for adventure, excitement, beautiful women," cried the young man to his father as he prepared to leave home. "Don't try to stop me, I'm on my way."

"Who's trying to stop you?" shouted his father. "I'll go with you."

"Nice teeth."

A young lady was permitted by her parents to take employment in a large city and live in her own apartment. The one condition was that she would not allow gentlemen friends to her apartment as it would worry her mother.

During a long distance phone conversation, the daughter described her date of the previous evening to her mother.

"You didn't permit that man in your apartment, did you?" queried the nervous mother.

"Oh, no!" replied the daughter, "we went to his apartment. Let his mother worry."

At a mountaineer's cabin way up in the mountain a very large family were seated around the dinner table and as is customary there was no passing of food. When they wanted something they just stood up and reached for it and some of the reaches were pretty long. One of the older boys was sitting at the table and wanted a slice of bread, so he stood up and stretched far across the table for it. The father sitting at the side wrinkled his brow and said: "Maw, how old is Zeke now," and Maw said, "Nigh onto twenty I reckon Paw," and Paw very seriously said, "Maw it appears to me we better start putting pants on Zeke. Did you see what he dragged through the soup?"

Henry and his over-developed wife were sitting in the stands waiting for the football game to begin. A friend walked over, said, "Hello Henry," gave his wife's breast a little squeeze and walked away. A few minutes later another guy walked over, said, "Hello Henry," fondled the wife's breasts and walked on. This strange sequence of events went on for some time. Finally a man sitting next to Henry spoke up: "Listen pal, it's none of my business but isn't it a little odd. At least twelve guys came by, said hello to you and then grabbed your wife by the breast. What's the story?"

Henry looked at him and moaned, "What can I do? If I leave her at home, she **sleeps** with everybody!"

"The party's been pretty much of a flop except for you two."

One doctor we know was perplexed by the case at hand. He had given his patient all sorts of tests, but his results were still inconclusive.

"I'm not sure what it is," he finally admitted. "You either have a cold or you're pregnant."

"I must be pregnant," his patient decided. "I don't know anybody who could have given me a cold."

By her boy friends a girl was
    called 'butter'
Though on oleo she had been fed.
When she asked, "Why the
    nickname?" they'd mutter,
"It's 'cause you're a much better
    spread!"

Down in the mountain country of the south they were trying a rape case and the victim was on the stand.

"Now, young lady," the prosecutor began, "please tell the court in your own words of your experience. First, can you identify the man?"

"That's the one," the girl pointed.

"And when did this occur?"

"As I remember, it was last June, July and August."

"Mildred! How **can** you after all we've meant to...Mister, will you please stop, while I'm talking to my wife."

"Did you follow my advice about kissing your girl when she least expects it?" asked the sophisticated college senior of his younger fraternity brother.

"Oh, hell," said the fellow with the swollen eye, "I thought you said **where**."

"Look, Herb! A full-breasted Chickadee!"

The little midget woman was complaining that she had a terrible pain in her groin whenever it rained or snowed. The doctor suggested that she come back to see him when the weather was inclement, which she did. He had her lie down for five seconds, then told her to get back on her feet and walk around a bit. "How do you feel now?" he inquired.

"Just fine, Doc," she answered.

"What did you do?"

"Oh," he replied, "I just cut four inches off the top of your galoshes."

Did you hear about the two queer judges that tried each other?

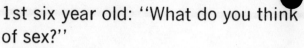

1st six year old: "What do you think of sex?"

2nd six year old: "It's a pain in the rear."

1st six year old: "You're doing it wrong."

The professor of criminal law was concluding his final lecture before the holidays: "Remember, gentlemen, if you have an affair with a girl under age, with or without her consent, it's rape; if you have an affair with a girl of age, without her consent, that's rape; but if you have an affair with a girl of age, with her consent, Merry Christmas!"

"There! See how easy it was to get a loan?"

"Well, here's your Paradise Island of beautiful man-hungry women!"

The wife came home with a brand new mink coat. Her husband said, "Where the heck did you get that?"

She replied, "I won it in a raffle."

The following night she walked in with a beautiful diamond bracelet. Again the husband asked, "Where the heck did you get that?"

Her reply was the same, "I won it at a raffle." Then she added, "And dear, would you do me a favor. I expect to go to another raffle party tonight and I'm in a hurry. Would you mind drawing my bath?"

The husband did as instructed but when his wife came in to take her bath, she found that there was only a half-inch of water in the tub. "Dear," she said, "Why didn't you fill the tub?"

"Well darling," he answered, "I didn't want you to get your raffle ticket wet!"

Two women were sitting in the doctor's waiting room comparing notes on their various disorders.

"I want a baby more than anything in the world," said the first, "but I guess it is impossible."

"I used to feel just the same way," said the second. "But then everything changed. That's why I'm here. I'm going to have a baby in three months."

"You must tell me what you did."

"I went to a faith healer."

"But I've tried that. My husband and I went to one for nearly a year and it didn't help a bit."

The other woman smiled and whispered, "Try going **alone,** next time, dearie."

"It...er...sleeps two."

"We're breaking up in 5 minutes, Folks—everybody back to their wives!"

The Martian landed his spaceship at a gasoline station that was closed for the night. Walking up to a gas pump, he demanded, "Take me to your leader." Receiving no reply, he stalked up to a second pump and repeated the question. Naturally the same thing happened. He went to the third, fourth and fifth pumps, got disgusted, hopped back into his spaceship and returned to Mars. Upon arrival, he reported to his Martian chief, "Those Earthlings are the worst. No one would talk to me; they're the most unsociable things I've ever met. But boy, are they hung!"

"My sister is the clever one," boasted Mike. "She pulled the wool over Uncle Sam's eyes. She got herself up like a man and joined the Navy!"

"Hold on there," protested Pat. "She'll have to dress with the boys and shower with them. Why' they'll catch her right away."

"Oh, you think so, do you," smirked Mike. "And who would be tellin' on her, eh?"

She was complaining to the doctor that her husband was too old for her and couldn't consummate the marriage. The doctor gave her some pills for her husband and left, promising him that she would let him know how things worked out. A week later, she came back and said, "Doctor, the pills were fine. For four days in a row, he did it morning and night."

"That certainly was an improvement," said the doctor.

She replied, "Oh yes! And just yesterday, he did it three times before he died."

A woman with a well-developed fashion sense knows that bare skin never clashes with anything she's wearing.

The recent survey on cigarettes found that 90% of the men who tried Camels . . . still prefer women!

"You'd think that they would get tired of hearing about her operation at every party!"

The clerk was signing in a new group of patients at the state asylum.

"Name," he asked one of the newcomers.

"Lord Chatteringham, if you please!" was the reply.

"That's OK by me," said the clerk. He assigned the man to a room; turned to the next man in line and asked him his name.

"Lord Chatteringham, of course," asserted the patient.

"You don't say," replied the clerk and assigned the man to the same room as the first chap, thinking it might prove interesting to have two Lord Chatteringhams together.

The next morning, the second fellow came to the desk.

"Sir, I lied last night," he said to the clerk. "I must confess. I'm not Lord Chatteringham at all. I am really LADY Chatteringham."

The hazy warmth of the summer evening provided an atmosphere of passion on the small lake, deserted except for a canoe drifting lazily on its surface. In it, locked in a warm embrace, lay Jack and Carolyn, looking soulfully into each other's eyes and whispering the special words of lovers.

With a delicious silken rustle that set the canoe to gently rocking, she pressed herself still closer to him. "Jackie," she breathed, "will you love me always?"

"Of course, my precious," he murmured tenderly. "Which way would you like me to try first?"

"Intermission!"

"What were his last words?"
"He said, 'I can't figure out how they can make anything on this stuff at a dollar a pint?'"

"Everything I have today I owe to my sweet, loyal wife...who died and left me three million dollars."

Then there was the prospective client who was extremely chagrined as he critically appraised his girl for the night.

"Girl?" he barked. "Girl?!? You must have spent your girlhood entertaining the Colonial Troops."

"**Please!**" the veteran prostitute replied with dignity. "Remember; mine is the **oldest** profession."

"I know," he moaned, "but I'll be damned if I'll spend the night with a charter member."

"Of course, that's only an estimate."

The husband finally cornered the Casanova who had been seducing his wife. "Look," he said, flourishing photos taken by a private detective he had employed. "Here's a shot of you and my wife in the living room of my apartment. Here's another of you drinking together, half undressed. And here's a picture of you two in bed together. Now, what are you going to do about it?"

The adulterer studied the photos carefully, nodding over each one. After a moment he picked up the third one and handed it to the husband. "All right," he said. "I'll take a dozen of this one."

The sign that's posted in each
   Greek bus
Sure fills the men with cheer.
They all obey it without a fuss
It says, "Step to the driver's rear!"

Now that I'm old and feeble
My pilot light is out.
What used to be my sex appeal
Is now my water spout.
I used to be embarrassed
To make the thing behave,
For every single morning
It would stand and watch me shave.
But now I'm growing old
And it sure gives me the Blues
To have the thing hang down my leg
And watch me shine my shoes.

"Is this the train with the Bar Car?"

"I hear you've been doing some experimenting over here, Harry."

Then there was the one about those two close pals, Pedro and Pancho. It seems that Pedro was getting married. So they had the usual beeg wedding feast, with much wine. Things were going fine, until Pedro missed his beautiful bride. Upon closer examination of the group, he found his pal, Pancho, was also among the missing. Naturally Pedro started searching the premises. Upon looking into the bridal chamber, he closed the door softly, and crept softly down the stairs to his guests, saying excitedly, "Queek, Queek, Everybody, come look...Pancho are so drunk, he theenk he are me."

"Darling," he breathed passionately. "Am I the first man to make love to you?"

"Of course you are," she snapped. "I don't know why you men always ask the same silly question!"

"Do you have anything that'll attract them yet make 'em keep their goddam hands to themselves?"

A pair of gossipy ladies seated on a crowded subway car happened to notice a very large waisted fat guy standing a short distance from them. The fat gentleman, having very good hearing, overheard their conversation.

"Mabel..." said one lady, "pick up on the belly on that character...if it was on a girl she'd be pregnant."

Answered the fat guy angrily:

"Look, lady. It was, and she IS!"

In a little village near Acapulco, Pedro the Pooped One was sipping a short beer in the local tavern when his friend Juanio rushed in.

"Pedro!" he shouted. "O blackest of all zee days! I just saw a man sneak into your hacienda and begeen making love to your wife!"

"Eez that so?" said Pedro calmly, continuing to sip his beer. "Was thees man very tall?"

"Si, si!" shouted Juanio.

"Be calm, amigo," cautioned Pedro. "Was he wearing a green coat and yellow sombrero?"

"Si, si!"

"And did he have a beeg black mustache?"

"Si, si!"

"Oh, that's Manuel. That fellow, he make love to ANYbody!"

A sad-looking guy appeared at the local police station and asked the officer in charge if he could swear out a warrant for the arrest of a star boarder living at his home.

"And what charge do you want placed against him?" queried the officer.

"Petty larceny," replied the guy promptly.

"Alright. Now, just what do you mean by petty larceny?" asked the cop.

"Well," stuttered the nervous guy, "it's this way. The boarder has been stealing my wife away from me— piece by piece!"

"What do you mean...it was an election bet? What does a young girl like you know about politics?"

"You've been married for 10 years, John, how come no children?"
"Well, to tell the truth, the night before I got married, I said to my bride-to-be, 'Look honey, we're getting married tomorrow. Why don't we go up to my apartment and we, uh, that is, uh—, I mean, uh—.' Well, she was so miserable that I've never asked her since."

A pretty young miss walked up to the bowlegged druggist and asked, "May I have some talcum powder, please."
He said, "Yes M'am, walk right this way."
She replied, "If I could walk that way, I wouldn't need any talcum powder."

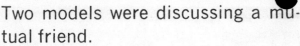

Two models were discussing a mutual friend.

"Gosh," said one, "can that guy dress!"

"Yeah," answered the other, "and quickly, too!"

A very fussy woman was in a restaurant and couldn't make up her mind what to order. The waiter tried to be helpful and said that they had some very nice tongue. "Do you think I would ever put anything in my mouth that had ever been in anyone else's mouth?" she asked.

The waiter thought a minute and said, "Why not try an egg sandwich?"

"Psst!...filthy pictures, Mister?"

"O.K. So sue me."

The three gals were recalling the greatest thrill of their lives.
"Mine," said the first, "was on my wedding night." The second said that her greatest thrill was when she first saw her first child.
The third gal, still unmarried, stunned her friends with this: "My greatest thrill happened when my cockeyed sister gave me an enema."

Hey, I got one of those new small cars.
Did you get a Falcon?
No, I got a good deal.

Two gay boys were out yachting when one accidentally fell over board and began to scream, "Save me! I can't swim, save me!"

His gay friend lisped, "Keep calm. Swim to that buoy!"

"Stop fooling around," shrilled the other. "I'm really drowning!"

With his wife out of town for the weekend the Casanova brought his girl friend home for a night's entertainment. Unfortunately, the young lady came unprepared so the guy looked around the house for the device his wife usually used. He came back empty-handed with the explanation: "I guess she doesn't trust me. She took it with her."

"...You're a disgrace to your uniform!"

Once two soldiers came across a dead animal and an argument began. One soldier said it was a donkey, the other claimed it to be a mule. An officer happened by and they asked him to settle it. He said stiffly, "It's an ass; Now dig a hole and bury it!" As the doughfeet were digging and grumbling, a pretty, little nurse walked by and asked sweetly:

"What are you two boys digging? A fox hole?"

The two soldiers grinned dryly and answered, "Nope!"

Did you hear about the girl who was picked up so often, she started to grow handles?

Wisdom: Knowing what to do.
Skill: Knowing how to do.
Virtue: Not doing it.

"...This is old stuff with you Edwards, but Miss Gompers I'm surprised at **you!**"

Gladys and Mildred were indulging in their favorite pastime, gossiping. Men were the principal topic and Mildred, who was plain by any standards, was doing most of the talking for a change.

"I tell you, Gladys," she bubbled, "he's the only guy in my whole life who's made me feel this way. The touch of his hand, the sound of his voice, oohhhhh. . . ."

"You sound pretty far gone on him," Gladys sniffed.

"Oh yes," said Mildred brightly. "This time it's the real thing. **SEX!**"

"What time did you get home last night, Dear?"

The old maid was walking down a dimly lit street when a holdup man jumped out of the bushes.

"Give me your money," he demanded.

"I d-don't have any," she managed to reply.

He proceeded to search her thoroughly. Every possible place of concealment was explored.

"I guess you were telling me the truth," he finally muttered angrily, "you don't have any money on you."

"For heavens sake," she wailed, "don't stop now. I'll write you a check."

He saw this beautiful creature at the bar, decided to ask her to join him for a drink. She said, "Okay, but it's not going to do you any good." They finished the round; again he suggested a drink. Her reply was the same, "Okay, but it's not going to do you any good." After finishing the second, he asked her for a dance. Again her reply was, "Okay, but it's not going to do you any good." They danced, returned to the bar; he looked at her and said, "Why don't we go to my apartment, have some drinks, order some food and listen to a little hi-fi, hmmmmm?" Like a broken record, she repeated, "Okay, but it's not going to do you any good."

They arrived at his apartment, had a little booze, a little food, were listening to some lovely music when he turned to her and asked, "Mind if I kiss you?" As expected, she replied, "Okay, but it's not going to do you any good." Getting desperate, he grabbed her and said, "Listen, you don't understand. We've been together now for over three hours. You're very appealing and I would like you for my wife!" Upon hearing this, she brightened up immediately and purred, "That's different. Send her up!"

He heard that a friend of his had passed away and felt he should pay his respects. Unwittingly he walked into the wrong house. There, in the living room, were six men sitting around. Imagining that he was in the right place, he sat down too. Just then, a beautiful, nude girl came into the room, undressed him and started making love to him. After fifteen minutes, he said, "It's been nice visiting you, dear. But let's hope next time we can meet under happier circumstances."

"Oh, **now** I remember why I called you . . . my husband is locked in the bathroom."

A traveling salesman was about to check in at a hotel when he noticed a very charming bit of femininity giving him the so-called "glad-eye." In a casual manner he walked over and spoke to her as though he had known her all his life. Both walked back to the desk and registered as Mr. and Mrs.

After a three-day stay he walked up to the desk and informed the clerk that he was checking out. The clerk presented him with his bill for $250. "There's a mistake here," he protested. "I have been here only three days."

"Yes," replied the clerk, "but your wife has been here a month."

"What does your husband do?"
"He works for the Humane Society."
"What's his job?"
"He runs the cat house."

The old man was saying to his doctor, "You know, Doc, when I was young, it was as hard as a rock. As I got older, I could bend it a little and now I can bend it a lot. Does that mean I'm getting stronger?"

"We have a very interesting service, Mr. Brady. If you feel like smoking, we send a man over to get drunk with you."

A recent independent survey indicates that it's still possible for a young woman with little or no experience to make her way into show business.

Wife: "Give me ten dollars. I want to buy a brassiere."
Husband: "What for? You've got nothing to put into it!"
Wife: "You wear shorts!"

"It's been a lovely day, Tom...please don't spoil it."

This gal had married the dreariest, lethargic bore in town and gone to Niagara Falls on their honeymoon. On their return she was all aglow with excitement.

"It was all so thrilling and wonderful!" she gushed.

Her friends, all of whom had dated the creep, listened with polite attentiveness.

One of the cats that couldn't take any more asked, "What happened? Did you go over the falls in a barrel?"

The husband dejectedly entered his home and told his wife that the doctor had informed him that he must stop working immediately. She took the news calmly and said, "Well, dear, you've supported me now for 42 years. The least I can do is go out, get a job and take care of you for a change."

"You're 68 years old," he said. "What can you do?"

"I'll find a way to bring home a dollar," she replied.

Three days later she returned home and gave her husband $60.10.

"How did you make all this money in three days?" he asked.

"I became a prostitute."

"At your age?" he shouted.

"Why not? I'm entitled!"

"But you made such an odd amount, $60.10. Who gave you the 10c?"

"Everybody."

"I'd like something that gives the idea I'm no cinch—But I can be had!"

Sweet Young Thing: "What are you thinking about?"

He: "The same thing you are."

Sweet Young Thing: "If you dare do anything like that, I'll scream!"

"I think **that's** the man that violated me, but maybe you'd better make him do it again so I can be sure."

The phone rang in the examination room and the young doctor answered. On the other end was the pretty young thing who'd been in earlier that day. "Oh doctor," she cooed, "would you please have a look around your office...er...you see, I think I left my panties there." Blushing furiously, the medico looked around the room, found nothing, then, just to be sure, looked under all the furniture in the waiting room, and reported back, "Sorry ma'am. Nothing here."

There was a slight pause on the other end of the line, then: "Oh, I suppose I must have left them at the dentist's."

The customer said to the waiter: "Give me a bowl of chicken soup please." The waiter returned with the order, his thumb immersed in the soup. The customer said nothing, ate the soup and a few minutes later asked the waiter to bring a bowl of hot borscht. Again the waiter returned with his thumb in the bowl.

The customer looked at him and yelled, "What's the matter with you! I asked for hot chicken soup; you put your thumb in it. I ask for hot borscht; you put your thumb in it . . . whaddaya, a smart guy?"

"I'll tell you the truth, sir," replied the waiter. "I have terrible rheumatism in my arm and it feels better if I keep it warm."

The customer was not impressed with the story. He glared at the waiter and said, "Why don't you take your thumb and shove it."

To which the waiter replied, "Oh, I do that when I'm in the kitchen."

"Man, you must **really** be hungry."

● Busy psychiatrist to nurse: "All right, send in that nymphomaniac and take the rest of the day off."

"What a pleasant bore! All she talks about is sex."

Wanda, a pretty but distraught model, took her troubles to a psychiatrist.

"Doctor, you must help me," she pleaded. "It's gotten so that every time a man takes me out, I wind up in bed with him. And then afterwards I feel guilty and depressed all day long."

"I see," nodded the psychiatrist. "And you want me to strengthen your will power."

"Heavens, no!" exclaimed the model. "I want you to fix it so I won't feel guilty and depressed afterwards."

He was complaining to his friend that he was losing his manhood. The friend suggested that he try eating rye bread every day. He ran into a bakery and ordered $20.00 worth of poppy seed rye. The baker said: "Twenty dollars worth? Why it'll get hard before you eat it!"

"In that case," he cried, "give me fifty dollars worth!"

The little cockney woman was asked how many children she had.

"Me and 'Erman, we 'ave twenty-six children!"

"Twenty-six children! My goodness, the Queen should give him a knighthood!"

" 'Twouldn't do no good. The bugger refuses to wear one!"

The evangelist was giving a fire and brimstone sermon against all the common evils and sins, covering everything from murder to petty gambling. One middle-aged woman sat in her camp chair swaying and rocking and frequently murmuring, "Amen, brother, amen."

The preacher, spurred on by her encouragement, started to exhort against whiskey drinking. "Amen, brother, amen. Praises be," encouraged the woman.

"And now," shouted the preacher, "I come to the worst sin of all! Those sinners among you who have fallen into loose sex habits must mend your ways."

The old lady stopped her swaying and commented hollowly, "Now he's stopped preaching and took to meddlin'!"

SICK! SICK! SICK!

"John! . . . The baby just fell out of the window!"

"Don't make me laugh when my lips are chapped."

"But, I don't like little brothers."

"You'll eat what I give you!"

"Mommy, Mommy . . . can I wear a bra? . . . I'm fourteen now."

"Shut up, Ralph!"

"I have a feeling that my husband is suspicious!"

For old men who want a renewal on life, they have a new hormone that works very quickly. The only trouble is, that you have to swallow it fast or you'll get a stiff neck!

Sandy Jamieson was a canny Scot. He knew how to stretch a dollar.

One of the amusing stories about him concerns his check-up visit to his doctor.

He carried with him a goodly amount of liquid specimen which the doctor examined in his laboratory.

"Everything's fine," announced the doctor, "couldn't find a thing wrong with your specimen."

"No sugar? No albumen?" asked Sandy.

"None at all," replied the doctor, "you're O.K."

Sandy grinned, and asked, "May I use your phone to call my wife?"

The doctor told him to go ahead and Sandy soon was talking to his wife.

"Good news, dear. Neither you or I or the kids or even Uncle Gordy have a thing the matter with us."

She had been dating one man steadily for almost a year, and her mother was growing concerned.

"Exactly what are his intentions?" she demanded.

"Well, Mom, I'm really not sure," replied the gal. "He's been keeping me pretty much in the dark."

"Why can't you spend a night out with the boys once in a while like other men?"

At a court hearing in the Ozarks a group of four boys were accused of contributing to Mary-Lou's delinquency. "Yes," Mary-Lou acknowledged, "Sam was one. And Bill and Joe were the others."

"But that's only three," the judge said. "How about Charlie, wasn't he there too?" "Oh sure," said Mary-Lou. "But Charlie is my cousin."

A farmer gathered his four sons around him and said, "All right, which one of you young'uns threw the out-house in the river?" No one said a word. The farmer continued, "Years ago, George Washington cut down a cherry tree. When his father asked him, 'George, did you chop down the cherry tree?' George replied, 'Yes, I did, Father.' His pa rewarded him. Now I repeat my question, which one of you young'uns threw the out-house in the river?"

His youngest son stepped forward and said, "It was me, Pop."

Whereupon, the old farmer took him over his knee and whaled the daylights out of him. The little boy looked at him through tear-filled eyes and said, "You told us George Washington got a reward after he confessed to chopping down the cherry tree."

The farmer said, "Yup, but his father wasn't **sitting in the tree when it happened!**"

Late for school, the kid gave his teacher this excuse:

"I had to make my own breakfast this morning."

"I don't believe you, but I'll take it up later. Right now, for our geography lesson...where's the Mexican Border?"

"He ran away with my mother... that's why I had to make my own breakfast!"

Frazzled wife in kitchen to homecoming husband ardently embracing her: "Why can't you come home exhausted like other men?"

"Oh, it's you—I thought it was just some salesman."

She was stretched out on her analyst's couch, looking voluptuous but unhappy. "Doctor, I just don't know what to do," she cried with feeling. "I can't help myself. Every night, no matter how hard I try, I end up bringing three or four men up to my bedroom. Last night, I had six. You've got to help me!"

"Yes," said the doctor sympathetically. "I know, I know, my dear."

"Oh," she exclaimed in surprise. "Were you up last night too?"

The old maid called the cops and said, "A sex maniac just broke into my house. Come and pick him up in the morning."

Two ladies were sitting on the beach in Miami. One of them decided to go for a swim. When she returned she put her hand down her bosom and withdrew a dry cigarette. Noticing the look of amazement on her companion's face, she explained:

"I have a great system. I place a cigarette in a rubber protective thing and it doesn't get wet. You can buy them at drug stores."

The following day, the second lady went into a drug store and asked the clerk if he had any protectors.

"Sure," said the clerk, "any particular kind?"

"Why, yes," replied the lady. "I want it to fit a camel."

"Oh, gosh! I forgot to bring my sleeping pills."

"If you don't keep busy you go crazy!"

A perennial bachelor had a ready answer for the inevitable question, "Why haven't you ever gotten married?"

"I was at a cocktail party one evening," he would reply. "It was very crowded and as I was trying to make my way across the room, I accidently bumped the arm of a beautiful young woman. She turned towards me with a really murderous expression on her face which melted into a smile when she saw who I was. 'Don't worry about it,' she said as I started to apologize. 'I thought it was my husband.'"

Two NYC call babes enter and seated themselves at a plush bar and the bar-jockey, without being asked, served them two bottles of their separate brands of beer. The girls were amazed and asked him how he'd known what they had wanted.

"Aw, I'm just a smart bartender, that's all," he replied.

"Baloney!" answered the gals, "you only guessed what we would order; you only guessed..."

"Oh, yeah? See that guy that just came in? He'll want a scotch on the rocks. Now watch, I'll go and ask him." The barkeep then walked down the bar and sure enough, the new customer ordered scotch on ice, to the girls' astonishment.

"Smart bartender, better believe it!" said the barman as he passed the girls again. A while later, when business slowed, the bartender leaned over the bar toward the two call girls.

"Look," he asked confidentially, "I've always wanted to ask this question. Can prostitutes ever get pregnant?"

"Why," quickly answered one of the girls, smiling at the other knowingly, "certainly they can. Where do you think all these smart bartenders come from!"

An airline recently introduced a special half-fare rate for wives accompanying their husbands on business trips. Anticipating many valuable testimonials, the publicity department of the airline sent out letters to all the wives of businessmen who used the special rates, asking how they enjoyed their trip.

Responses poured in asking, "What trip?"

"How would you like to be the love interest in the book I plan to write about this experience?"

A rather flamboyant blond sailed through the door, into the room, without knocking, and demanded, "Doctor, you must speak frankly and tell me what is wrong with me."

"My dear madam," said the man sitting in the room. "I can sum up your difficulties in three sentences. First, you are too fat by twenty pounds. Second, you have far too much paint on to be attractive. And third, I am an artist. The doctor is on the floor above."

"I own more stocks than any guy!"
He bragged to each one of his pals.
Yes, he had a finger in each pie
Till he found it's more fun with gals.

During an interview, a famous screen beauty was asked by a reporter about her literary preferences.

"What would you take along to read if you knew you were going to be marooned on a desert island?" was the way he put it.

"A tattooed sailor," was the quick reply.

"Martha! The ransom note specifically said —'don't try to find me or notify the police.'"

A man called the undertaker and cried, "Come over and bury my wife."

"But," said the mortician, "I buried your wife ten years ago."

"I got married again," sobbed the man.

"Congratulations," said the undertaker.

A man owned a male parrot that he had become exceedingly fond of.

The parrot had become despondent and after all sort of experiments to snap him out of it, he deduced that his feathered friend needed some sex.

A beautiful female parrot was located in a pet shop and a deal was made to have his bird serviced for $50.00.

The female was delivered to his apartment and placed in the male parrots cage. Instantly, the male let out a terrifying scream and tore at the females feathers. "What are you doing?", screeched the female. "For fifty bucks, honey," shouted the male, "I want you nude."

"Sold American!"

A little boy and girl squirrel were chattering and playing around when up comes a fox. The girl squirrel dashed up a tree but the boy squirrel stayed on the ground.

"That's strange," said the fox. "Usually squirrels are afraid of me and run up the nearest tree."

"Listen bud," replied the boy squirrel. "Did you ever try to climb a tree when you were in love?"

Preacher finding two boys masturbating: "You keep that up and you'll go blind!"

First boy to second: "Let's just do it 'til we need glasses."

"What happened to you?" he asked his friend with the swollen, black eye.

"I called my girl friend a **two bit whore.**"

"Golly, what a shiner, what did she hit you with?"

"A bag of quarters!"

"I'll be a little late dear. I stopped off on the way home for a short one."

He called his doctor and began shouting hysterically, "My five-year-old son just swallowed a contraceptive!"

"Don't worry, I'll be right over."

As the doctor was about to leave his office, the phone rang and the same caller announced, "Forget it Doc, I found another one!"

"Stop worrying about it passing the censors. There's no film in the camera anyway."

"Yes, my daughter finally got married. I hated to lose her; she was such a lovely, charming girl. And I am not at all happy with the big mouth that she married."

"Why?"

"Well, he's such a boisterous individual, so loud in everything he does. Even at the ceremony, when the minister asked him, 'Do you take this woman to be your lawful wedded wife?' he shouted, 'Yeah, yeah, I'll take this broad.' He yelled so loud that my poor sweet daughter almost had a miscarriage!"

Mildred is so seldom in her cups that she's forgotten what size she takes!

The office vamp reported, "I went out with a millionaire from Detroit last night, and what do you think he gave me? Five hundred dollars!" "Wow," jeered the girl at the next desk. "That's the first time I heard of a $498 tip!"

Arriving home unexpectedly from a business trip, the husband found his wife in bed with his best friend, in what may be described as a compromising position.
"See here," shouted the husband, "just what do you two think you're doing?"
"See!" said the wife to the man beside her. "Didn't I tell you he was stupid?"

"What did you use for bait?"

The pretty young thing was waiting her turn to register at a motel when she overheard the desk clerk tell the man in front of her that he'd just gotten the last room. She waited for the gentleman to leave the desk and then approached him.

"There isn't another motel within miles of here and I'm dead tired," she pleaded. "I figure it this way; you don't know me, I don't know you, they don't know us, we don't know them. How's about me spending the night with you?"

The man, a rather dopey looking character, said, "I don't care. Com'on."

They went to his room; he started to disrobe and so did she. "Listen," she said, "you don't know me, I don't know you, they don't know us, we don't know them. Let's have a few drinks. I got a bottle." After they'd gotten a little high, she cuddled up to him and whispered, "You don't know me, I don't know you, they don't know us, we don't know them . . . let's have a party!"

He looked at her in astonishment and cried, "For heaven's sake! If I don't know you and you don't know me and they don't know us and we don't know them . . . who the hell are we gonna invite!"

While the fashionable Parisian world passed by their table, Jacques explained the plot of **Lolita,** which he had just finished reading, to his friend Michel.

"It is an amazing book," said Jacques to his sophisticated friend. "It tells the story of an affair between a middle-aged man and a twelve-year-old!"

"Alors," exclaimed Michel, "a twelve-year-old **what?**"

"Yes, dear, the car door will be fixed today. As a matter of fact, I'm waiting at the body shop right now."

A big Kansas farmer found it necessary to go to Minneapolis for several months and decided to leave one of his best workers in charge. "I want you to take care of things, Hank, as if I were here myself. Understand?" Hank nodded.

Four months later the boss farmer returned to find everything in shape. Said Hank, pointing things out, "the chicks have been laying plenty of eggs, the wheat has grown double strong, the vegetables are better than they've ever been, and as for those monthly spells your daughter used to have, I've even got those stopped."

"All right lady," said the bill collector, "how about the next installment on that couch?"

The lady shrugged. "Better than having to give you money, I guess."

"I take it back—your secretary isn't at all stuffy."

The father, passing through his son's college town late one evening on a business trip, thought he would pay his boy a surprise visit. Arriving at the lad's fraternity house, dad rapped loudly on the door. After several minutes of knocking, a sleepy voice drifted down from a second floor window, "Waddyah want?"

"Does Walter Bradshaw live here?" asked the father.

"Yeah," replied the voice. "Dump him on the front porch."

A marriage broker was trying to arrange a match between a business man and a beautiful young girl. But the business man was very cagy.

"Before I buy goods," the business man said, "I look over samples, and before I get married I must also have a sample."

"But good heavens man, you can't ask a respectable girl for a thing like that," the broker replied.

"Sorry," insisted the other, "I'm strictly business and I want it done my way or not at all."

The broker went off in despair to talk with the girl. "I got you a fine fellow," he said, "with lots of money. But strictly business he is and he don't do nothing blind. He must have a sample."

"Listen," said the girl. "I'm as smart in business as he is. Samples I won't give him; references I will!"

"Ouch!"

"Please don't inhale so quickly."

Said the worried patient to the psychiatrist: "I'm in love with my horse."

"But that's nothing," replied the psychiatrist. "A lot of people love animals. My wife and I have a dog that we love very much."

"Ah, but doctor, it's a physical attraction that I feel toward my horse!"

"Ummmm!" said the psychiatrist. "What kind of horse is it? male or female?"

"Female of course!" the gent shot back angrily. "What do you think I am, queer?"

An oversexed lady named White
Insists on two dozen a night.
A fellow named Chedder
Had the brashness to wed her—
His chance of survival is slight.

"That's odd—I would have sworn I saw you come out here with young Rockinshaw."

The young soldier wrote his first letter home: "Dear Pop, I can't tell you where I am but yesterday, I shot a polar bear."

A couple of months later came another letter: "Dear Pop, I still can't say where I am but yesterday, I danced with a hula girl..."

Three weeks later came still another note: "Dear Pop, still can't say where I am but yesterday, the doctor told me that I should have danced with the polar bear and shot the hula girl!"

Did you hear the one about the gorgeous secretary who left her clothes at the office and took her boss to the cleaners.

"What do they call intercourse in outer space?"
"Outercourse!"

Definition of voluptuous: A woman who has curves in places where some girls don't even have places!

"I had a wonderful time...unless the check bounces, of course."

One wife to another, "Don't worry about your husband flirting. My dog chases cars, but if he caught one, he wouldn't know what to do with it."

"He's too old to be **buying**—He must just be **looking**."

The friend said, "I can't help it, George, your wife attracts me physically something fierce and if I could just pinch her on her backside just once, I'd give two thousand dollars!" "For that kind of money," said the husband, "I don't think my wife would object. Go ahead, pinch her." The wife leaned over a chair, exposed her backside and the friend looked long and hard. Finally, after about five minutes, he said, "I just can't do it."
"Why not," inquired the husband. "Haven't you got the nerve?"
The friend replied, "No, I haven't got the money."

The mother took her son to the psychiatrist and complained that he was continually thinking about sex. The doctor drew a square on a piece of paper, looked at the boy and asked, "Son, what comes to your mind when you see this drawing?"

The kid answered, "Looks like a window."

The doc said, "What do you think is going on behind that window?"

"People are behind that window," replied the kid. "They're huggin' and kissin' and makin' love."

The doctor then drew a circle and asked, "What comes to your mind when you see this?"

The kid said, "That's a porthole."

"And what do you think is going on behind that porthole?" inquired the doctor.

"Oh," said the kid, "there's people behind that porthole, with their clothes off, drinking, making love and having a ball."

The doctor said, "Son, would you mind leaving the room. I'd like to discuss this with your mother."

The child got up to leave and as he reached the door, he turned around and said, "Hey Doc, can I have those dirty pictures you drew?"

Herb got into work late one morning and immediately announced to the office gang, "What a screwball I met this morning." Pressed for details, he told this story:

"This morning my wife and I overslept. I woke up about nine o'clock, dressed quickly and was just ready to leave when the bedroom door opened." "Who was it?" someone asked. "The iceman," Herb answers. "Boy, can you imagine a guy being so dumb that he comes into the bedroom looking for the icebox?"

"Why, yes—I believe Mr. Holzapple is expecting you."

"Did you see that donkey fall on the street yesterday and break his leg?"
"Did they blame the driver?"
"No, they said it was the asphalt."

It was sundown, and the young athlete was doing push-ups on the beach when a drunk appeared. The drunk weaved his way to within a few yards of the perspiring young man, sat down on the sand and laughed and laughed. "What in the devil are you laughing about?" asked the annoyed young man. The drunk laughed and laughed, and then sputtered, "Don't look now, but shumbuddy sthole yur girl."

Did you hear about the Sunday School teacher who chased her boyfriend all over the church and finally caught him by the organ!

First author: What did you title your new book?
Second author: Sex after death, or how to be laid in a coffin!

"Oh, well, you can't expect everything!"

"Have you heard about the guy that fell into the cesspool — he couldn't swim but he went through all the movements!"

When asked the difference between a snow man and a snow woman, the little boy replied, "Snowballs!"

A couple, married for thirty years, had never missed a night of connubial bliss. Not feeling well one day, the wife consulted her doctor and was informed by the medico that she must have complete rest and quiet for six months or she would not live.

The wife and husband decided that they must stay completely apart during this period. She moved into an upstairs bedroom and he remained downstairs.

After three months of complete abstinence and solitude, his will power collapsed and he started for her bedroom. Just as he was about to ascend the stairs, he saw her coming down. Their eyes met and she said, "Dear, I was just coming down to die." To which he quickly replied, "I'm glad honey, because I was just going up to kill you."

Doctor to call girl: "You're run down. I advise you to stay out of bed for a week."

Martha and Abe had been married for some time and to Abe's chagrin, Martha no longer had as much enthusiasm as she had once for fun and games in bed. One night, not long ago, when Abe was making love to her, he suddenly said, "Is something wrong? Are you hurt?"
"Of course not," snapped Martha. "Why do you ask?"
"Oh," replied Abe wistfully, "I just thought for a moment there, that you moved."

"Reflexes . . . good!"

"Ethics are vital to the successful business man," a successful business man told his young son. "For example, an old customer paid his account today with a hundred dollar bill. As he was leaving the shop, I discovered that he had given me two hundreds, stuck together. Immediately a question of ethics arose: Should I tell my partner?"

"SHAME! BAD DOG, REX! NAUGHTY! NAUGHTY!!"

The crippled old man hobbled over to the soda fountain and in a feeble voice, said to the clerk, "May I have a chocolate sundae, please?"
The clerk looked at him and asked, "Crushed nuts?"
The old man replied, "No, just rheumatism."

Everyone looked up as the couple walked through the restaurant to their table. She was young, beautiful and voluptuous while he was old, haggard and stooped. The waiter came over to take their order and the young woman proceeded to order the most expensive dishes in the house. Her escort was somewhat staggered and asked, 'Do you eat this well at home?''

"No," she replied, "but then, no one there wants to sleep with me!"

"Fred! he asked for a drink of **water**."

Helen: "I don't see why you want to marry Jack. He's just an every day sort of fellow."

Mary: "Well, any girl should be satisfied with a man like that!"

A timid, rather elderly man employed in the local pickle factory had for years the driving urge to insert his finger in a pickle slicer. One day he returned home early from work all happy and elated, and quite naturally his wife asked him what was the matter.

"Well, doggone it! I done it...I finally went and done it!" said the man.

"What did you do, for Heaven's sake?" asked the wondering wife.

"Put my finger in a pickle slicer! That's what I did, damn it!" blurted out the elderly guy.

"Well, then," asked the wife, "what did they do to you for doing it?"

"Aw!" replied the man, "they fired me, that's what they done."

"And what about the pickle slicer, may I ask?" queried the wife.

"Oh," grinned the husband, "they fired her, too!"

"I should never have let him rehearse the Honeymoon!"

The husband wired home that he had been able to wind up his business trip a day early and would be home on Wednesday. When he walked into his apartment, however, he found his wife in bed with another man. Furious, he picked up his bag and stormed out; he met his mother-in-law on the street, told her what had happened and announced that he was filing suit for divorce in the morning.

"Give my daughter a chance to explain before you do anything," the older woman pleaded. Reluctantly, he agreed.

An hour later, his mother-in-law phoned the husband at his club.

"I knew my daughter would have an explanation," she said, a note of triumph in her voice. "She didn't receive your telegram!"

A recently-hired maid came to her employer one afternoon and explained she would not be able to come to work the next day: "My little boy's sick with the measles."

"Your little boy? Why, Martha, I thought you told me you were an old maid."

"I am, but not one of the fussy kind."

The girl selling tickets at the railroad station was built like she was designed by a sex fiend. The nervous male customer couldn't keep his eyes off her bust.

"Will you stop staring at my bust and tell me what city you want a ticket to?"

"I'm not staring at your bust. Just give me two plicketts for Tittsburg!"

"The guests are starting a game of Charades...better hurry or you'll miss all the fun."

A woman vacationing in the country last summer saw a young boy coming down the road leading a huge and recalcitrant bull.

"Where do you have to go with that bull?" she asked.

"To service a cow down the road," said the struggling boy.

"Couldn't your father do it?"

"No, it's got to be the bull."

Why is it that men praise women for their virtue and dislike them so when they try to keep it?

A little boy went to school for the first time and the teacher explained that if he wanted to go to the washroom he should raise two fingers. The boy, looking puzzled, asked—"How's that going to stop it?"

A man engaged a prostitute and throughout their night's tryst he kept exclaiming: "Phooey! Phooey!"
The girl became offended at this apparent slur on her professional ability, and when her part of the bargain had been concluded, she asked, "Why did you keep saying 'Phooey'? Wasn't I good enough for you?"
"Don't get me wrong," the guy said quickly. "YOU were fine. When I said 'Phooey,' I was thinking of my wife."

After a night of celebration, he woke up to find himself in bed with one of the ugliest women that he had ever seen. He looked at her and said, "Who the hell are you?"

She replied, "I don't know who I am now but last night you told me that I was the Yellow Rose of Texas."

The modern young miss was being chided by an archaically minded aunt for smoking. "Smoking is a disgusting habit," she lectured. "I'd prefer being caught at adultery than found with a cigarette dangling from my lips."

To which, the modern girl replied with a laconic "Who wouldn't?"

"He's engaged to a girl in Dallas!"

A little boy rushed up to his next door neighbor and cried, "Lady, did you see a white poodle puppy-dog that peeped in, pooped and popped out again?"

She answered, "No, but I'd like to catch the cat that creeped in, crapped and crept out again!"

"Let's play grownups. I'll be Mommy and you be the Salesman that comes every day."

A certain senator, it seems, had to visit Chicago recently for a Committee Hearing and wanted to take a female acquaintance along.

"I have senatorial immunity," proclaimed the senator, "so you needn't be afraid of the Mann Act."

"Afraid of it?" she giggled. "Why, Senator, I just adore it!"

A bra manufacturer who sells his product under the slogan "Every Girl Wants EMBARGO" was asked why he picked "EMBARGO" for a trade name. "At first glance you may think it's foolish," he explained, "but spelled backwards, it has tremendous sales appeal."

After delivering Mrs. James of her ninth child, the doctor called the husband aside.

"Next time you feel like propagating," he said, "ask yourself if you can support another child."

"Doc," replied James, "when I feel like propagatin' I feel like I could support the whole state of Georgia."

MARRIAGE
COUNSELOR

"...I'm in love with him, he loves me, we both enjoy the same things, he earns plenty of money, we're real happy together....My problem is; what shall I tell my husband?"

"Well, here's luck!"

Once upon a time, as the story goes, on a Christmas eve many years ago, Santa Claus made the bizarre error of descending the wrong chimney into a brothel. "Won't you stay a while?" purred one of the girls, her negligee slipping to the floor.

"I'd better be going," the Old Boy grunted, clutching his toysack.

"Oh, **please** stay a while—please?" She peeled off her stocking.

"But I'm Santa Claus, and I have presents to deliver," he insisted.

"Surely you can spare me a FEW minutes, Santy?" She wriggled toward the bed.

"Well—," he said finally, "I might as well, seeing that I couldn't get up the chimney anyway."

Fran: "How do you feel after going out with a fellow who has no sense of humor?"

Martha: "Wonderful—I never knew you could have lots of fun without laughing!"

Seated at a table in one of those intimate little French restaurants off Broadway, the young couple were studying the unfamiliar items on their menus.

"I never know what to ask for in these places," the man said.

"Ask for an ambulance," groaned the gal, "here comes my husband!"

I think every man should have a hobby, and this is mine.

The unemployed actor came home after a day of visiting booking offices. His apartment was a shambles and his beautiful young wife was lying on the bed in hysterics. It was obvious that her clothes had been literally torn from her body.

"What happened?" shrieked the actor.

"Oh, darling!" she sobbed, "I fought and fought, but he......"

"Who did this awful thing? Who was it?"

"He came here looking for you. He said it was very important. Finding me alone and defenseless he......"

"Who? Who?"

She hung her head and in a husky voice replied, "Your agent."

"My agent!" the actor's face beamed. "Has he found a part for me?"

The frightened young man was sitting in the induction center, waiting to be examined. His friend walked out of the examiner's office and said, "Well, I'm 4F."

"How did you do it?"

"I showed the doc the truss I was wearing and he said, '4F'."

The young man said, "Gee, let me borrow the truss. Maybe I can fool him too." He put on the truss; walked into the doctor's office; the doctor examined him and said, "Egypt."

"Egypt!" protested the young man. "But Doc, I've worn a truss for nine years, nine solid years!"

"My boy," replied the doctor, "anyone who can wear a truss upside down for nine years, can ride a camel."

"OK, you're hired," said the busy executive, moving around his desk toward the buxom young female. "Now would you like to try for a raise?"

"Now how about one for the road, dear?"

The mother was complaining to the doctor that her son was continually masturbating. The doctor asked the boy, who was sitting there, "Why do you do it?"

To which the boy replied, "'Cause I'm bored. There's nothin' to do. I don't like TV and I hate baseball, so I masturbate!"

The doctor sent the boy to the waiting room while he discussed the situation with the boy's mother. Ten minutes later, they went into the waiting room themselves and found the place strewn with candy wrappers.

"What have you been doing?" asked the doctor in amazement.

"Eatin' these candies," replied the boy.

"What?" said the doctor. "I had a five pound box of candy here. Do you mean you ate the entire box?"

The boy said, "Sure, I was bored; I had nothin' to do."

"Nothing to do!" shouted the doctor. "You little jerk, why didn't you go home and masturbate!"

Getting married is a good deal like going into a restaurant with friends. You order what you want, then when you see what the other fellow has, you wish you had taken that.

The husband put down his magazine, looked at his wife and said, "I see that in Brazil the women pay the men seven dollars each time they make love to them. It's too good to pass up, I'm leaving on the next boat." The wife shouted, "I'm going with you." "What do I need you for?" he shot back. She countered with, "I just want to see how you are going to live on $14.00 a month."

"I love my wife and hate my mistress."

"My parents forbid me to see you. What gets me is how you built up such a bad reputation in the short space of four years!"

Bob's sister was one of the most popular girls in Manhattan. She had more boyfriends than she knew what to do with and she never wanted for a thing. Bob was always in debt and constantly asking his sister for spending money.

"I don't understand you, Bob," she said in obvious annoyance one afternoon when he had tried to put the bite on her for a 10 spot. "I don't have any trouble saving money, so why should you?"

"Sure, sure," he said, "but you've got money coming in all the time from the very thing that's keeping me broke."

Bed-wetting had plagued Roscoe from childhood. He was filled with shame but couldn't seem to control himself, no matter how hard he tried. Finally his wife had all she could take and ordered him out of the house until he was cured.

Roscoe went to the doctor who advised him to see a psychiatrist since his chronic bed-wetting was probably due to a mental or emotional disorder.

About three weeks later, he returned home wearing a cheerful face. His wife met him at the door and cried, "Honey, you look so happy. Are you cured?"

"Nope," replied Roscoe, "but now when I wet the bed, I'm PROUD."

"Honey, I think Junior's finally outgrown his fear of girls."

Beatnik character to druggist: "Hey man, got any aspirin, cha, cha, cha?" Druggist: "No, but I have some Ex-Lax, poop, poop, a-doop."

MARRIAGE LICENSES

"If we're too young for a license, how about a learner's permit?"

The husband had a hunch that his wife was cheating on him but wasn't quite sure. He hired a detective to follow her and received the following report: "They started out to dinner at eight o'clock, went to a night club and then went to his apartment. The lights went on in the living room, then I could see them in the den, and finally the lights went on in the bedroom for about five minutes. They started to kiss and hug and she began to disrobe." The husband grew very excited and demanded to know what happened next. The detective said, "Well, at that point the light went off."

The husband sighed and said, "See what I mean, always that element of doubt!"

This little guy was in a bar, hoisting a few, when he was approached by a young lady, who asked him to dance. He said, "I'm no Fred Astaire, but I'll dance." While dancing she said, "Will you buy me a drink?" He replied, "I'm no 'Rockefeller,' but I'll buy." Upon downing the drink, she looked at him and said, "Would you care to come up to my room for an hour or so?" He said, "I'm no Kirk Douglas, but I'll go." They left for her apartment, and after spending an hour there he proceeded to put on his jacket to leave. She looked at him and asked, "Hey, wait a minute. How about some money?" He looked at her and exclaimed, "I'm no gigolo, but I'll take it!"

"Do you cheat on your wife?" asked the psychiatrist.
"Who else?" answered the patient.

"Now don't do something that will make me hate you, dear."

Bank Clerk (to young lady): "Awfully sorry ma'am, but this twenty dollar bill is counterfeit."
Young lady: "Dammit, I've been seduced."

"Hello, Acme Bakery?..."

At one of those cocktail parties, the talk turned to the matter of sterility and the great number of childless couples. One young wife boasted that she could have a baby "at the drop of a hat."

"What's holding you back?" jibed someone.

"Oh, you know darn well that my husband's away on business," blushed the young wife.

"And he took the hat with him," sarcasmed a grinning bachelor.

The young widow was so sure the rich young man-about-town was father to her out-of-wedlock child that she brought a paternity suit against him. The man-about-town defended himself vigorously, insisting he had had nothing to do with the event.

During the trial, the judge asked him, "Tell me, did you ever sleep with this woman?"

Quickly, unhesitatingly, the playboy snapped, "Not a wink, Your Honor, not a wink!"

A pharmacist found it necessary to leave his drugstore one day. He asked his soda clerk to keep an eye on things until he returned. No sooner had the pharmacist left than in staggered a lushed-up character demanding in a loud voice some medicine to cure his hiccups.

The druggist returned and asked if there had been any customers and the soda clerk replied:

"Only one, a drunken guy with a bad case of the hiccups."

"Well," asked the druggist, "did you tell him to come back when I was here?"

"Oh, no," answered the kid soda jerker, "I took care of it myself. I mixed him up a cup of Epsom Salts with Citrate of Magnesia, Castor Oil and Mineral Oil; then I gave him some ExLax to nibble on. He took it right then, too."

"Great Scott!" said the druggist, turning pale, "that mixture won't stop the hiccups!"

The soda clerk smiled knowingly and said: "Want to bet? Take a look outside; there he is holding on to that lamp post afraid to hiccup!"

Bellhop at the 'Hit and Run' Hotel. (Making a fellow and lady comfortable) "Anything else, sir...?"
Guy: "No, that's all. Thank you."
Bellhop: "Anything for your wife...?"
Guy: "Why, yes. Come to think of it. Bring me a postcard."

"For goodness sake, Harry, TIP him!"

The ventriloquist who visited the farm amazed the local yokels with his ability to throw his voice into the various animals. One of the farmers walked up and asked, "Can you make all those animals talk?"
The ventriloquist replied, "Yes, all of them."
The farmer leaned over and whispered in his ear, "Well, if that sheep on the end says anything about me, it's a dirty lie!"

"What do you mean you'd like to try her out for size?"

Her name was Chloe and she was curved like the road up Pike's Peak. Alas, she also was virtually brainless. But fortunately, this was no drawback as far as Henry's plans for the evening were concerned. He was delighted when she agreed to come up to his apartment for a nightcap.

As he prepared the drinks, full of anticipation, Chloe explored the apartment, stopping now and then to examine a painting or book title, she didn't quite understand. At last she stopped dead in front of his fireplace.

"What on earth is that?" she asked pointing to a carved, wooden object lying on the mantel.

"Oh, that. It's African," he replied. "They use them in their fertility rites. It's a phallic symbol."

"Humph," sniffed Chloe demurely. "I'd hate to tell you what it looks like!"

Husband, upon meeting ex — after two years of separation, "Listen honey, why don't we have a few drinks, dinner, go to my apartment and really make love?"

Ex—: "Over my dead body!"

Husband: "You haven't changed a bit!"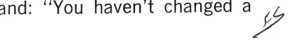

"I thought I gave you till sunset to get out of town."

A salesman was looking for his buddy, a George Sexhour. He entered the hotel; walked up to the girl at the desk and asked, "Do you have a Sexhour here?"

She replied, "Mister, we don't even get a coffee break!"

The Sultan had ten wives.... Nine of them had it pretty soft.

Bud did you hear about the legal secretary who told her amorous boy friend: "Stop and/or I'll slap your face."

EVERINGHAM

"Boy what a lousy party...I got so drunk I ended up in bed with my own husband."

A middle aged business man took his wife to Paris. After walking all over the city on a shopping tour he begged off for a day to relax.

Once rid of the old gal he visited a few bars and finally picked up a pretty hustler. He was having a ball until she brought up the subject of money. She asked for fifty and he offered ten. She refused to bargain and so they didn't get together.

That evening he took his wife to a good restaurant and there he spotted his pretty companion of the afternoon seated at a table near the door.

"See, monsieur?" said the babe, as they passed near her table. "Look what you got for your lousy 10 dollars."

Have you heard the one about the lament of the pregnant ballerina? "I should have **danced** all night!"

Three young French boys from Paris were spending their summer on a farm in Normandy. One day, as they were walking by a hay field, they caught sight of the milk maid and the farm hand in the hay stack and stopped to watch.

"Ah," said the seven year old, "look at the grownups fighting."

"You are in error, my friend," replied the sophisticated eleven year old. "They're making love."

"Yes," agreed the thirteen year old, "but rather amateurishly."

He held her close against him, a warm glow of satisfaction covering them both.

"Am I the first man you've ever made love to?" he asked.

She studied him reflectively. "You might be," she said. "Your face looks very familiar."

"Yes, it's mine...but I'm still paying nightly installments on it."

The two loaded gentlemen stood at the bar near closing time.

"I've an idea," said one, "lesh have one more drink and then go find us shum girls."

"Naw," replied the other. "I've got more than I can handle at home."

"Great," replied the idea man, "then lesh have one more drink and go up to your place."

Hymie, there's a mouse. I heard it squeak!
So what do you want? I should get out of bed and oil it.

"Can you change a twenty?"

Girl explaining her cynical view of life:
"We were out on his yacht when he told me a big blow was coming, so like a damn fool I let him tie me to the mast!"

The Wac went in to see the Medical Officer and said, "Doc, I need an operation."
He asked, "Major?"
She replied, "No, corporal."

The newlyweds had been married the day before and this was their first breakfast together. Shyly, the bride spoke. "Darling, I have a confession to make. I should have told you before. I suffer from asthma."

"Thank Heavens," cried the groom, "and all the time I thought you were hissing me."

A big radio network once took a twenty-three year old reporter as a foreign correspondent. Believing his age to be a hindrance to the dignity usually afforded a foreign correspondent, they released the boy's age as twenty-nine. The boy's hometown newspaper picked up the story and displayed it prominently. Unfortunately, on the same day the story appeared there was an equally prominent display on the following page announcing that the boy's parents were celebrating their twenty-fifth wedding anniversary.

A Union organizer went to a bawdy house and he appraisingly looked over the girls. "There," he said to the matron, "I'll take that one," he pointed to a cute little blonde number.

"Oh, no you don't," said the matron. "You'll take that one over there," and she pointed to an old haggard looking girl who sat alone in a corner. "She's got seniority rights."

The young salesman was boasting to the head of a big insurance company that he was the best salesman in the world. When asked to prove it, he went out and sure enough, he came back with a deposit on a fifty-thousand dollar life insurance policy. The president was impressed and said, "By the way, did you get a specimen?" The salesman didn't know what he meant so the president explained that for medical reasons, a specimen was required from each new applicant for a policy. The salesman went out and came back a short time later with two buckets **full.** When asked what this represented, he replied, "Well, the fellow that I sold the policy to originally, was in a board meeting with twelve other guys and I figured I'd kill two birds with one stone so I sold them a group plan."

"I'd like a piece of that, myself."

First Old Man: I've had a wonderful life on Earth, and I know my time is coming. When I pass away, I'd like to be buried beside George Washington because he stood for everything fine and decent.

Second Old Man: When I pass away, which should be soon, I'd like to be buried next to Lincoln. That would make me feel very happy.

Third Old Man: Well, when I go, I'd like to be laid down beside Marilyn Monroe.

First Old Man: But she's not dead yet.

Third Old Man: Neither am I!

A young man called on a sixteen year old girl, and remarked to her parents that he was from Philadelphia.

The girl's father commented that he and his wife were married there seventeen years ago. A startled expression passed over the man's face. Next morning the daughter said in disgust, "That certainly did it, Father. I had told him I was eighteen; so then of course, I had to tell him I was illegitimate."

He: "Just think, I've never had a lesson in my life."
She: "It's darn nice of you not to blame it on somebody else."

"On guard, Miss Brown . . ."

The admiral had made himself very un- popular and when he fell ill and had to go to the base hospital, everyone breathed a sigh of relief. The hospital did not im- prove his temper, however, and he made life miserable for the staff. One day, one of the orderlies put on a surgeon's mask and went into the admiral's room, picked up his chart and examined it very profes- sionally. Then he advised the admiral that he would have to take his temperature and told him to roll over onto his stomach. On no account was the admiral to turn over and he promised to return to read the thermometer as quickly as possible. The admiral harumphed but did as he was told.

About an hour later, the floor nurse looked in to check on the admiral and found him still on his stomach. "What on earth are you doing, sir," she cried.

"What's the matter with you," growled the admiral. "You've seen people having their temperatures taken before."

"But Admiral," she cried, "with a DAF- FODIL?"

A salesman returned home after a year on the road to find that his wife had been untrue to him. "Who was it," he demanded, "was it my friend Al?"

"No," answered his wife.

"Was it Joe, or Sam?" asked the hus- band.

"No," answered the faithless wife.

"Was it my friend Harry?" he asked in a tone of misery.

"Whatssamatter?" screamed the wife, "Don't you think I have my own friends?"

"You'll be able to recognize me easy. I'll be wearing a black-eyed susan in my button hole!"

It was the first day for Marie, the newly hired salesgirl in the maternity shop and it had been hectic. From the moment the store opened, it had been jammed with customers and Marie had sped from one to another without stopping. Now, just as she concluded a large sale and expected a breathing spell, the doors opened and a fresh flood of very expectant ladies poured in.

"Good heavens," the exhausted salesgirl cried in anguish. "Doesn't **anyone** do it for fun any more?"

Confucius says, "Woman who cooks carrots and peas in the same pot . . . very unsanitary."

It happened in the bridal dept. of a large store in Minneapolis. A customer staggered the usually imperturbable bridal consultant by asking to see "maternity wedding gowns." "Sorry," gasped the flustered man, "but I doubt that you'll find a garment like that in all of Minnesota." "It's about time then that you people woke up around here," rejoined the woman. "They have them in Kentucky!"

"We can't go on meeting like this, Gloria."

The young Jewish boy, on the telephone, kept hollering, "Operator, operator, I can't hear my party."
The operator answered, "I'm sorry sir, but you've been cut off."
The Jewish boy said, "I know but it shouldn't affect my **hearing.**"

"No, he's not my father ... He's my husband!"

It was six years since Alfred had visited his home town. In that time, he had gone to Hollywood and become a successful screen star. His old friends were eager to hear of his experiences and gathered around the night of his return to learn about life in the film capital.

"Most of the stories you hear about Hollywood and film people are so much tripe for publicity," Alfred informed them. "It's a hard working place, and being a film star isn't much different from any other job. You get up and go to work and when you are through you return to your home. I'm almost never up later than ten o'clock. Why, only the other day, I said to my bride, "George......""

He was a wealthy, elderly bachelor and like all Frenchmen, he was fond of the ladies. Despite his age, he continued to fulfill his gallant obligations to the fair sex. He lived in Montmartre, in a small, private residence which was full of objects d'Art and rare antique furniture.

Each evening he returned home with a lady companion, and each young lady, upon examining the priceless works of art would ask:

"But to whom will all these lovely things be left?"

The old rogue always replies:

"My will mentions that everything here will be left to whomever is with me at the time of my death."

The old rake has some truly wonderful nights!

When the husband left for work, his four year old son said to his mother, "When you're not home, Mommy, Daddy takes the maid upstairs and —." His mother stopped him, saying, "Tell me the rest when your Daddy gets home tonight."

At dinner that night, she said, "all right, Bobby, you may finish your story."

"Well, last Sunday, when you weren't home," lisped Bobby, "Daddy took the maid upstairs and did to her what you and Uncle Charlie do when Daddy's gone fishing."

The eighty-six year old man while talking to his doctor, said, "I've a confession to make. About four weeks ago, I picked up an eighteen year old girl, took her to a hotel and we made love all night long. Three weeks ago, I picked up a twenty year old girl, double parked in front of her house, made love for four hours. Just last week, I grabbed a seventeen year old girl, took her to the park and we've been making love for six straight days."

"My goodness," gasped the doctor, "picking up all these strange girls; I hope you're using some **precaution!**"

The old man chuckled and replied, "Oh sure, I give them a phoney name and address."

Secretary sitting on boss's lap: "Your wife isn't the only one. Frankly, no one in the office understands you either!"

If you drive after you've been drinking, make sure you've got a car.

Henry was helping his son fly a kite in the back yard, but was having trouble getting it to stay up. His wife stood watching them from the porch. Henry had just run the entire length of the yard, trying to pull the kite into the air, only to have it thrash about uncertainly and plummet to the ground.

"Henry," said the wife, "you need more tail."

"I wish you'd make up your mind," said Henry, panting heavily. "Last night you told me to go fly a kite!"

"Stick to your carrots and lettuce and hop in to see me next month!"

"Three fifths of 100 proof bourbon—Oh yes, a bottle of 86 proof for the children."

It was late at night when the doorbell rang and the Madam wearily slipped on a kimono and went to the door. She was surprised to be confronted by a man with both arms and both legs in plaster casts.

"I'd like a woman," he said.

"Look," she replied compassionately, "why don't you just go home. It's late and I'd like to get some sleep."

"I'd like a woman," he repeated.

"Let's be realistic," she said pointedly. "What could you do with a woman in your condition?"

"Listen, lady," he replied, "I rang the bell, didn't I?"

The elevator was very crowded and two elderly women were squeezed into the back. The first old woman said to the other, "Mabel, the fellow behind me, is he good looking?" Mabel replied, "Well, he's young." "I know that," snapped the other. "I want to know if he's good looking."

"Come right over, Mother—Frank and I had our first quarrel."

A couple of farmers were returning from the local saloon one afternoon when they spotted a lamb stuck in a barbed-wire fence.

"I wish it was Jayne Mansfield caught in that fence that way," said one of the drooling men.

Replied the other, "I just wish it was dark!"

"I shouldn't be serving you wine. You are head of the Temperance League," said the charming hostess.

"Oh, no, I'm chairman of the Anti-Vice League."

"Well, I knew there was something I shouldn't offer you."

A wolf lounging in a hotel lobby perked up when an attractive lady passed by. When his standard "good evening, dear" brought nothing more than a frigid glance, he sarcasmed:

"Pardon me, I thought you were my mother."

"I couldn't be," she replied icily, "I'm married!"

"Soon as she started working here, I knew it was only a matter of time before the 20 year partnership of Donahue and Smith would end."

"Will you please stop saying 'TWO WITH EVERYTHING' every time a couple of girls walk by."

It happened in the hills of Tennessee. A local wife had just given birth to her twelfth child, and as she was leaving the hospital with her latest in her arms, her nurse good-naturedly remarked, "Well, I guess we'll be seeing you next year just about this same time."

"No you won't! That's fer sure," she answered confidently.

"Well, how do you know?" the nurse asked.

"Becuz me an' m'man jest found out whut's causin' 'em."

An Indian drank 62 cups of tea. The next morning they found him dead in his tee pee.

It isn't the hop, skip and jump that's responsible for wearing out the rug between twin beds — it's the slow drag back!

The two shipwrecked men on the deserted island had decided to pass away time by playing a guessing game with movie stars.

The first one started off: "I am five foot five, long blonde hair, passionate green eyes, a 40" bust measurement, 23 inch waist. I am sultry, and very appealing, with large luscious lips. Who am I?"

"I don't care who you are!" exploded the second fellow—"kiss me quick!"

AJAX COLLEGE

"The quotation happens to be 'all men are created equal', not 'all men are made the same.'"

"Roger has turned into a real old stay-at-home."

The old lady was sitting in her rocking chair, feeling so lonely, and thinking to herself, "Oh, if I only had youth again and could be beautiful, I wouldn't ask for anything more." Just then a genii appeared. He said, "Old lady, your wish will be granted." He touched her with his magic wand and she was transformed into a beautiful girl. The genii said, "and because you have been so good on earth, you are hereby granted another wish." Looking down at her cat that was by her side, she replied, "Turn my cat into a handsome prince." It was no sooner said than done. She rushed into the arms of the handsome prince, exclaimed, "Oh, this will be heavenly." The prince looked at her and replied, "Boy, will you be sorry you took me to the Vet."

Once there were twin brothers named Jack and Jim. Jack was married and Jim was still single but the proud owner of a dilapidated old boat. Disaster struck them both on the same day; Jack's wife died and Jim's boat sank. A few days later, Jim met a friend on the street who mistook him for Jack and offered his sympathies, saying, "You must feel terrible!"

Jim replied, "Oh, not really. She was an old wreck from the beginning. Her bottom was all shrivelled up and she smelled like dead fish. The first time I got in her she made water faster than anything I've ever seen. There was a bad crack in her back and a pretty big hole in the front. The hole got bigger everytime I used her and she leaked like crazy. But what finished her was, these five guys I know borrowed her. I told them she wasn't very good but they said they'd take a chance with her anyhow so I rented her out. Then the crazy fools tried to get into her all at once and it was too much for her. She cracked right up the middle."

At this point the friend fainted . . .

A definition of slipcover: A maternity dress.

A five year old boy had a terrible habit of sucking his thumb; a habit his mother had been trying desperately to break. She told him that if he kept on sucking his thumb, he would blow up and burst. A few days later, his mother's bridge club came over. One of the women was very much in the family way. The little boy wandered into the room, looked at the pregnant woman and said in a loud voice, "Say, I know what you've been doing!"

"...And what else wouldn't your mother allow you to do as a child!"

Little Mitchell hurt his finger and ran bawling to his mom.

She kissed it and said, "There, there son, it'll feel better now."

Later in the day he showed up with a bruised nose, swollen eye, bleeding elbow, skinned shin, and sprained ankle — in that order. And each time his mother kissed the tender area.

Just before bed-time he once more came running for succor to his mother, screaming wildly and pointing to a more intimate region of his anatomy.

"Oh no you don't," his mother said. "Damn it, you're getting more like your father every day!"

Maybelle was at lunch when the hold-up men arrived at the insurance company where she worked. The thugs had forced all the girls to remove their dresses and lie on the floor.

When Maybelle entered the room and witnessed the scene she lost no time in taking off her dress and joining them. "Turn over, Maybelle," said the girl on her right, "this is a stick-up, not the office party."

"I warned you that bringing your wife along would ruin the hunting trip."

Man to druggist: "How much for prophylactics?"
Druggist: "Three for 50c."
Man: "Give me one."
Druggist: "Why only one?"
Man: "I'm trying to break the habit!"

Miami Beach lifeguard to hotel guest: "I've been watching you for the last three days, Mr. Gallstone, and you'll have to stop urinating in the pool."

Mr. G.: "Everybody urinates in the pool."

Lifeguard: "From the diving board?"

The squeaking of the bedsprings increased in intensity. Then, silence. Her quiet voice broke the stillness of the darkened room.

"I'm not myself tonight," she insisted.

"Well, whoever you are," he sighed, "it certainly is an improvement."

Mary and Bob were in their upper berth on the train to Niagara Falls, and she was so wonderstruck that she kept repeating over and over again: "Bobby, I just can't believe that we're really married."

Finally, a sleepy voice bellowed out from below: "For chrissake, Bobby, convince her — we wanna get to sleep!"

"Take me to your leader!"

"I'd like to buy a brassiere."
"What size?"
"Six and seven-eighths."
"That's ridiculous. There is no such size."
"Don't tell me, it fits right over my head!"

"Fred, I've been meaning to talk to you about a separation!"

The husband was complaining to the doctor that his wife was too amorous and was ruining him physically. The doctor suggested that he make himself unattractive and smear himself with some horrible smelling substance. Three days later, the husband returned and the doctor asked him how the plan had worked out. "Well," said the husband, "I smeared myself with limburger cheese and now she chases me into bed with a bottle of beer and a pumpernickel!"

Definition of good, clean fun: A couple taking a bath together!

The handsome young man walked into a drug store that was operated by two old maids and said, rather sheepishly, "Everytime that I see a woman, I want to hug and kiss her. and make passionate love. What can you give me?"

The one old maid leaned over to the other old maid for a brief consultation and then replied, "My sister and I will give you five hundred dollars and the drug store!"

"Just WHAT do you mean, 'be a good scout?'"

Guy: "I'm a bachelor."
Gal: "It must be terrible to grow old and not have someone love you."
Guy: "Yes, that's why I never married."

"Ugh!"

They were crushed together in a passionate embrace when John decided that the psychological moment had arrived to tell Marsha.

"Darling," he murmured, "I think you're a marvelous person and I want you to know that I certainly appreciate your-ah-company, but as far as I'm concerned, marriage is for squares."

Marsha replied with a small sigh of pleasure.

"What I mean," John continued doggedly, "is you're more like a sister to me."

At that Marsha's eyes opened in surprise and she exclaimed, "Good Lord, what a home life you must have!"

One of the ironies of life is that it's usually the warm girls, not the cold ones, who get the fur coats.

But withal and whatever, it must be realized that even the members of the oldest profession—or, to paraphrase Arthur Conan Doyle, "The Scarlet League"—are, in the final analysis, just people like the rest of us. They are born, and they pass on, just like the rest of us. And they have a certain kinship—just like the rest of us.

So it came to pass that when one of the girls of the Establishment died, the funeral was a beautiful affair. Hundreds of friends and clients showed up for the solemn procession. Car on car of brightly colored flowers followed the slow moving hearse, and when they finally arrived at the cemetery the Madam took her place at the side of the yawning grave and began to weep copiously. Two of the girls, standing nearby, heard the Madam muttering through her sobs—a quiet, reflective, eulogy: That was a wonderful girl. She brought in more business than any girl I ever had. She was the best prostitute I ever knew.

One of the girls turned to her companion. "See?" she mused, "You have to die before they say something nice about you!"

"I'm looking for a present," said the customer to the store clerk. "It's for my very old, very rich aunt. Any suggestions will be appreciated." The clerk thought for a moment and then came up with, "How about some floor wax?"

"Could I borrow a cup of Gin, neighbor?"

First Woman: I heard your daughter got married.
Second Woman: Thank goodness!
First Woman: I heard she had a baby.
Second Woman: That's nature, isn't it?
First Woman: Three months after the wedding?
Second Woman: Well, she's a very young girl. She just didn't know how long to carry it!

"Let me remind you I'm a married woman, Mr. Hutchens—pull down the blinds."

Two old men met two charming old ladies at a summer resort. They decided to have a double wedding ceremony. Immediately after, they retired to their respective rooms and they didn't meet again until the following morning, when they compared notes.

"Boy," said the first old man, "What a night I had with my bride. Three or four times. By the way, how did you do with yours?"

The second old man hesitated and then replied, "To tell the truth, it slipped my mind completely."

Definition of a race track: A place where windows clean people!

The difference between war and peace is that there has never been a good war.

"Henry, we can't go on meeting like this."

Percival surprised his set by announcing one night in his rather high, nasal lisp, that he intended to get married the following Tuesday. Some of his more skeptical acquaintances made bets that he wouldn't go through with it but to their surprise, he even went on a honeymoon trip.

When he returned, one of the heavy losers accosted him and asked in a sarcastic tone. "Well, Percival old chap, is your wife pregnant?"

"I do hope so," lisped Percival. "I really shouldn't want to go through **that** again!"

"We'll have to meet some other way. My husband is getting suspicious of me getting arrested for cattle rustling every night."

Three young boys were playing in the street of a London slum. A Rolls Royce stopped and a beautiful, expensively dressed blonde stepped out. She crossed over to the boys, picked up the youngest, hugged him and left a box of candies, and filled his hands with money. Waving good-bye, she re-entered the car and departed. The other boys were goggle-eyed.

One said, "Blimey, Jackie, was that yer fairy godmother?"

Jackie looked at him with scorn and replied, "Naw, that wuz my sister wot was ruined."

The Broadway chorus girl was exuberant over receiving a role in a forthcoming play.

"I was made for the part!" she crowed happily.

"Shhh," cautioned her friend, "you don't have to tell everybody."

"P-ss-ss-tt-!!"

A guy kept propositioning his girl friend and she kept refusing. He used all of the usual arguments, plus a few new ones, but to no avail. In a last desperate bid, he threw the whole book at her. "Listen, honey," he pleaded, "we're in love and soon we will be married. And in the eyes of God I'm sure we are already man and wife. Really now, I don't think you can give me one good reason why we should wait."

She replied that she could think of three good reasons.

1. "I'm a good decent girl."
2. "We are not married till we see the preacher."
3. "Besides, it always gives me a headache."

Two young movie actresses met in a studio during the lunch hour, and one complained to the other that she had been troubled for quite some time with vermin. "How can I get rid of them?" she asked.

"Just rub in some Paris Green," advised her friend, "that'll kill 'em."

A few weeks later they met again and the friend asked: "Did you get the Paris Green?"

"Yes," replied the other.

"Did it kill the lice?"

"I'll say it did—and also two directors and the leading man."

"My mother," said the sweet young secretary, "says there are some things a girl should not do before 20." "Your mother is absolutely right," replied the suave advertising manager. "I don't like a large audience either!"

"I wish you'd start your attack...the suspense is maddening!"

The son meets his father coming out of a house of ill-repute. "Pa," he said, "You? In a place like this?"
The old man looked at him and replied, "I'll tell you the truth, son; I refuse to argue with your mother for five dollars."

When wine, women and song begin to exhaust you; give up singing!

An English visitor to Charleston, South Carolina, decided to pick up a few American shirts. He asked his taxi driver to stop at the first haberdashery he saw. "Yes Sir!" said the driver, but when stopped by a red light inquired, "What was that you said boss?" "A haberdashery," repeated the Englishman. "Yes Sir!" said the driver. They rattled along for a few more blocks and then stopped again. "Listen, boss," the driver exclaimed, "with me there's no beating around the bush. What is it you want? Liquor or women?"

A prominent New York physician was visited by the wife of a wealthy Japanese business man. Her marriage was childless and she had come to the doctor's office in the hope that he could help her. The doctor, who had a reputation for gruffness, ordered her to take off her clothes and lie down on the table. The woman paused a moment, sighed, and then as she started to disrobe, she said, "Very well, if it is necessary, doctor. But I HAD wanted a Japanese baby."

Two gay boys were listening to a wife and husband having a big argument, when one of the gay ones turned to the other and said, "I told you these mixed marriages never turn out well!"

Mr. Goldberg, a prosperous furrier, sent his daughter to Europe to get some culture and maybe meet a rich fella.

A few months later she wrote and asked papa to send her a book on etiquette.

"Real fine people she's meeting," he thought to himself.

Five months later she wrote for another book on etiquette.

"Princes she's going with," said Goldberg, and jumped for joy.

Having been away two years, Becky came home! Mr. Goldberg met her at the pier and was taken aback when she appeared with a child in her arms.

"Whose baby?" he asked.

"Mine," she replied.

"And the father?"

She shook her head. "I don't know, papa."

Goldberg wept in despair. "Two books on etiquette you got and you don't even know to ask, 'With whom have I the pleasure'?"

"Don't worry. She's bound to shrink a little during the cooking."

"That reminds me: Where were you last night?"

The little boy was out in the back yard with his chemistry set. He seemed to be driving nails into a board. His father approached and asked, "What are you doing with those nails?"

The son replied, "They're not nails, Dad. They're worms. I apply some of my secret formula to these worms and they get as hard as nails."

The father said, "Make me some of that stuff and I'll buy you a new bicycle." The kid was thrilled and gave his father a small bottle of the formula. Two days later, sure enough, there was a new bicycle outside the house and beside it, a beautiful motor scooter. The kid hollered, "Thanks for the new bike, Dad, but who's the motor scooter for?"

His father replied, "That's for you too, son. It's a present from your mother."

There was an old lady who lived in a shoe,
She had so many children she didn't know what to do,
Evidently!

"I know what I'm talking about. He's every inch a king."

We're sure you've heard about the traveling salesman whose car broke down in a rain storm. He ran to the closest farm house and knocked on the door. A grizzled old farmer answered and the salesman pleaded for a place to stay the night.

"I can give ya a room," said the farmer, "but I ain't got no daughter fer ya to sleep with."

"Oh," said the salesman. "Well, how far is it to the next house?"

"...This area through here is known for its interesting, spellbinding mirages!"

Three prosperous but aging industrialists were sunning themselves in the patio of one of Miami Beach's most expensive hotels. "Now that we can afford it, it's hard to enjoy it," one of them said. "Here I am in this beautiful place with all these gorgeous women around and my eyesight is so bad I can hardly make out the surroundings."

"I know," said the second. "It's my stomach that's failing me. I could order lobster, but I have to eat spinach. I love champagne, but I must drink milk."

"Yes," the third man agreed. "I've got a problem, too. Just last night I asked my wife to roll over and she said, 'What! Not again, Harry. We just finished the third one fifteen minutes ago.' You see, with me it's memory."

The old man was informed by his doctor, "Your hearing is getting worse and you must cut out smoking, drinking and women." The old man replied, "What, just so I can hear a little better?"

"We're looking for a den mother!"

Fellow entered almost empty Bar and ordered a whiskey sour and told the barkeep to fix up the other lone guy at end of bar a drink also. Finishing his first drink the fellow called the bartender and said:

"Give me another of the same, eh? But this time leave the fruit out of it."

"Why, you go to Hell!" screeched the guy at the end of the bar. "I never asked you for a drink in the first place!"

"Look, buddy, you torture them your way, I'll torture them mine."

The night before, he was really polluted. In the morning he rolled over and there beside him in bed was a truly ugly woman, sleeping peacefully. He got out of bed quietly, dressed, left twenty dollars on the bureau and started to walk out when he felt a tug at his pant leg. He glanced down and there was a woman who was even uglier than the one in bed. She gazed up at him and said, "Nothing for the bridesmaid?"

Mother: (Putting her four year old son to bed.) "Shhhh! The sandman is coming..."
The Kid: "Give me a quarter and I won't tell Daddy."

Then there's the one about the thrifty tom cat who put a little in the kitty every night.

"Not here, Wunjab—they might see us. Remember that palomar telescope on earth—?"

The Earthman, walking on Mars, came across a beautiful girl stirring a mixture in a huge pot. "What are you doing?" he asked.

"I'm making babies," replied the lovely Martian.

He said, "Let me show you the way we do it on Earth," and he proceeded to demonstrate. At the conclusion, she inquired, "Where's the baby?"

"Well," said the Earthman, "That takes nine months."

"Oh," asked the Martian, "Then why did you stop stirring?"

A house maid had been working for her employer for two years. One day she said, "Mrs. Smith, I'm pregnant and having no husband, I don't know what to do."

Her employer, being a kindly woman, said, "Don't worry dear, have the child and I will adopt it."

A year and a half went by and the maid approached her employer, saying, "Mrs. Smith, I'm with child again."

Her employer was annoyed but didn't want to loose the girl's services, so she adopted the second child too. Three months after the birth of the second baby, the maid came to the woman and said, "I'm sorry Mrs. Smith, but I must leave. I couldn't possibly work for a woman with two children."

A Presidential candidate was campaigning in the West and was giving a speech at an Indian reservation. "If I am elected, my friends, my party will love you as our neighbors." "Buzzonga! Buzzonga!" cheered the Indians.

". . . and we will eliminate war, poverty and disease!" he continued. "Buzzonga! Buzzonga!" thundered the Indians, the excited squaws holding their papooses in the air to better see the speaker. "We will teach all citizens to have tolerance and understanding . . ." kept on the candidate. "Buzzonga! Buzzonga!" roared the tribe in tribute to the white man's ending his speech.

Later, while talking to the Chief, the politician noticed an odd breed of horses grazing in a nearby field. Explaining his interest he asked if he could walk among them and look them over.

"Sure, you can," replied the Chief, "but be careful that you don't step in the Buzzonga!"

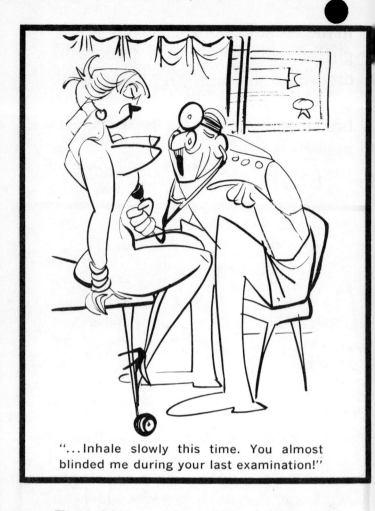

"...Inhale slowly this time. You almost blinded me during your last examination!"

The older gentleman took his young, voluptuous wife to see the psychiatrist. Overwhelmed by the wife's sexiness, the doctor threw her on the couch and began making mad passionate love to her. After a few minutes, the doctor turned to the husband and panted, "Your wife needs these treatments very badly. You must drive her down to my office every Monday, Wednesday and Friday."

The husband scratched his head and replied, "Well, I dunno, Doc. Monday and Wednesday I can drive her down here but I'm afraid on Friday, she'll have to take a bus."

In the cocktail lounge, a lovely young girl seated herself at a table and ordered a drink. The waitress went back to the bar and whispered to the bartender, ''Does she look old enough to you?''

''For what?'' asked the bartender.

''But Sir!...you just said 'no fraternizing with the **women.'** On this planet, these are the men.''

Mountain Preacher: ''Is thah any among you bredren that has had some experience with ghosts?''

Sam: ''I has.''

Preacher: ''What kind of experience, brother?''

Sam: ''Intercourse.''

Preacher: ''You mean to say you-all had intercourse with a ghost?''

Sam: ''Ah beg yo' pahdon,'' he replied. ''Ah thought you said GOAT.''

"That man you assigned to shadow my wife is no longer shadowing her...he's ACCOMPANYING her!"

Two ragged beatniks were sitting on a small pier in the Florida Everglades, dangling their feet in the stagnant water. Suddenly an alligator swam up and snapped a leg off one of them.

"Hey, man," the unfortunate fellow said to his buddy, "like an alligator just bit off my leg."

"Which one?" asked the cool friend.

"I dunno, said the first cat. "You see one alligator, you seen 'em all."

First man to second man: Where are you running to, John?

Second man to first man: It's the children's night out and I've got to get home and take care of the maid.

Then there was the chap who said there was only one thing that would turn his stomach. That was a nice warm pair of breasts at his back.

"I could never marry you, Henry...you lack imagination, for one thing!"

"We're going down!" The captain
   shouted
"And we've got no time to lose!"
Cried Miss Ella Strong, "I knew all
   along
This was just another pleasure
   cruise!"

"But Mother, none of the other fellas have to wear high heeled shoes."
"Shut up, for heaven's sake! We're almost at the draft board!"

"The doctor will be here just as soon as he warms his hands."

The mother got on the train with her six children. When the conductor came by for her tickets, she explained, "Those two are 12 and have to pay full fare, but these two are nine and the other two six-and-a-half, so they only pay half rate."

The conductor scratched his head and as he punched her tickets, he said: "Excuse me for asking, madam, but do you get two every time?"

"Oh, no," she said. "Sometimes we don't get any at all."

New cocktail for the tense executive: Take one jigger of Vodka, then fill up the glass with milk of magnesia. It's called a phillips screwdriver!

"You didn't hear right—I ordered striped bass!"

The elderly gentleman was nearing eighty but refused to accept his loss of sexual desire and stamina. He consulted with his doctor.

The doctor was amused and asked "Why should you be so concerned? It's expected at your age."

"But," pursued the oldster, "a friend of mine who is eighty-five says he makes love to his wife every night."

The doctor smiled. "Well, can't you say the same thing?"

He: What's the matter? Don't you love me any more?

She: Of course I do. I'm just resting, that's all.

A couple on a blind date visited the carnival grounds at a local park. They went for a ride on the merry-go-round. The ride completed, she seemed kinda bored. "Now what would you like to do?" he asked. "I'd like to be weighed," she replied. So he took her over to the weight guesser. "107," the man said—and he was absolutely right.

Then they rode on the whip, after which he again asked her what she would like to do. "I wanna get weighed," was again her answer.

"There's a screw loose here somewhere," thought Paul, so he took the babe on back home even if it wasn't yet ten o'clock.

And the gal's mother, noting that she was home unusually early, said to her, "What's the matter, Dear? Didn't you have a good time?"

"Wousy," came back the answer.

"Last week it was a mink coat!" roared the playboy when he saw the latest acquisitions his beautiful gal displayed for his approval. "This week it's a diamond necklace, five hats and ten dresses!"

"So!"

"So where do you think I am going to get the money to pay for these things?" Raved the playboy.

"That's your affair," rejoined the chick. "I'm not going around with you to give you advice on financial matters, am I?"

"Behind every successful man is a woman.
I couldn't afford her if I weren't..."

The newlyweds were suffering from exhaustion and after an examination, their doctor advised, "It's not unusual for young people to overdo things during the first weeks of marriage. What you both need is rest. For the next month I want you to limit your sex to those days of the week with an 'r' in them. That is, Thursday, Friday and Saturday."

Since the end of the week was approaching, the newlyweds had no immediate difficulty following the medico's orders. But on the first night of scheduled rest the young bride found herself eager as a beaver. Hubby fell asleep, but she tossed and turned and finally nudged her spouse into partial wakefulness.

Expecting daylight, and confused with the darkness, he asked, "What day is it?"

"Mondray," said his bride, cuddling against him.

"They sure are."

The minister was asking his congregation to donate as much money as they possibly could for the new church. Suddenly the town's **Lady of the evening** spoke up and said, "Reverend, I'd like to donate twenty-five hundred dollars!" The minister replied, "As much as we need funds, I refuse to accept tainted money."
A male voice in the back of the church shouted out, "Take it, Reverend. It's our money anyway."

One husky Beatnik to another after a rumble: "Man! What a dirty fighter he is. Did you see him swing his crutch at me?"

The young housewife called her grocer and told him how much her husband had enjoyed the canned meat. The grocer said, "Madam, if it's what I think it is, it's **cat food.**" The housewife replied, "Well, he doesn't seem to notice the difference and it's agreeing with him, so keep on sending it over."

Two months and one hundred cans later, the grocer called her on the telephone and inquired, "How's your husband?"

The housewife answered, "Up until last week, he was all right. But then one night he jumped up on the piano and while trying to lick his groin, he fell off, broke his neck and died."

"Do you like girls?"

"Remember, now, if my wife shows up... you start typing!"

The drunk asked where he could find a house of ill repute. He got the right number but remembered it wrong and tried to get into a home where a woman was leaning over the sink washing dishes. The drunk rushed over, threw her on the floor and began making love to her. Her husband, in an adjoining room, heard the rumpus. He ran to the kitchen, grabbed the drunk and proceeded to beat him to a pulp before throwing him out the door. The drunk looked up at him from the driveway and said, "Boy, you sure got a lot to learn about running a bawdy house!"

An acquaintance of ours, a used car dealer, informed us that he's had to change his sales pitch. It seems in this age of cynicism the little old lady who only drove on Sundays has given way to the nymphomaniac who only uses the back seat!

Newly weds, the groom aged 75 and his bride of 22, just arrived at a resort hotel. The next morning all the hipped guests were curious and they all managed to make breakfast.

Presently the 75 year old groom came romping down the stairs like a playful child. Very cheerfuly speaking and nodding to everyone in sight, he called the waitress and ordered six scrambled eggs, eight slices of toast, juice, etc., which after being served was attacked with gusto.

A half an hour later, the 22 year old bride shuffled slowly down into the dining room amid curious stares and seated herself at the table. The bride's eyes were sunken into her head and encircled with large dark rings; her cheeks were haggard and she wore a strange, vacant look on her face.

The new husband brushed her lips with barely a kiss and excused himself to use the telephone for a business call.

The waitress who could contain her womanly curiosity no longer went over to the new bride at the table and asked:

"Look, honey, I know it's none of my business, but you look something terrible, all worn out...what on earth happened?"

The 22 year old answered wearily: "I went with him for five years and he always was the perfect gentleman, only he kept telling me that he'd been saving up for forty years and I thought he meant money!"

"Look, Pierre! How many times do I have to tell you, in this country we ask for the lady of the house, not the house madame."

The elderly woman walked into the liquor store with two guns, pointed them at the owner and said, "Give me six bottles of scotch, all the money, and I want you to take me into the back room and make love to me."

He got the money and he got the scotch; then took her into the back room where he proceeded to make love to her, her guns still pointed at his temple. In the excitement of the lovemaking, the woman dropped her guns. He paused momentarily and said, "Lady, would you mind picking up your guns again; I'm expecting my wife any minute."

The college psychology class was studying human reaction to sexual stimulus and of special interest was the frequency of amorous relations.

"How many students here," said the professor, "engage more than once a week?"

Five people raised their hands.

"And how many engage once a week?"

Ten hands went up.

"How many twice a month?"

Eight hands went up.

"Once a month?"

Four hands were raised.

"And how many once a year?"

A little guy in the back waved his hand frantically and giggled hysterically.

"If you engage only once a year," said the professor, "I don't see what you're so overjoyed about."

Flushed with excitement, the little guy said, "Yeah, but tonight's the night!"

"I have to go to the bathroom."

"You're fired, Miss Karlson—turn in your falsies!"

The farmer was busy working in the south forty when his little son, Johnny, came running out to tell him that a man had just driven up to the house in a big automobile.

"Johnny," said the haggard farmer, "run back to the house as fast as your legs will carry you and ask that man what type of work he does. If he says he is a traveling minister, run down the cellar and lock up my liquor cabinet. If he says he is a law officer, lock the garage where I keep the still. If he says he is a salesman—sit on your ma's lap until I get there...."

If all the world loves a lover, why are there hotel detectives?

The director was having difficulty with the amateur actor with whom he was rehearsing a summer show.

"You've got to put timing and feeling into it," he said.

"Take that line where you enter and say, 'Cleopatra, Cleopatra, what have you done?' Stop after Cleopatra and take a couple of short breaths and then put some umph into 'What have you done?' Get it?"

The aspiring actor nodded. They regrouped the players, and set the scene again. Then he re-entered:

"Cleopatra," he said, "Cleopatra (sniff, sniff), what have you done?"

When the hotel detective had assured himself that a guest on the sixth floor had an unregistered person sharing his room, he reported his findings to the manager, who picked up the housephone, got the man on the line and without much ado asked him if his guest was a lady. "Hold the line," came the brash reply. "I'll ask her."

Three girls were considering what kind of man they'd prefer being shipwrecked with on a desert island.

"I'd want a guy who was a wonderful conversationalist," mused the first.

"That'd be O.K.," said the second, "but I'd rather have a man who could hunt and cook."

The third smiled and said, "I'd settle for a good obstetrician."

The young man had given his fiance a parrot for a birthday present. The first evening when she was disrobing in preparation for her shower, the parrot ogled and said, "Pretty, pretty blue panties!" A very smart bird, thought the girl—he even can distinguish color.

The next evening, the same thing happened with pink panties. "Pretty, pretty pink panties!" said the parrot. I've got an unusual bird, thought the girl.

The next evening as she headed for the shower, without even panties, the parrot squawked, "Pretty, pretty, pretty . . . and how are you fixed for blades?"

Girl in theatre: "The guy next to me is masturbating!"
Girlfriend: "Ignore him."
"I can't; he's using my hand!"

If you've enjoyed this book, you'll be more than delighted with others in the series...

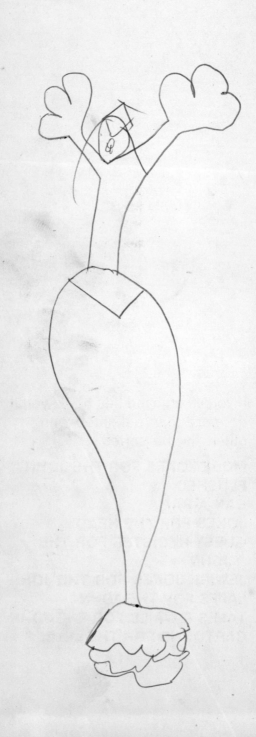